FOLLOW THE LEAD

Surviving Today's Market That
Lives and Dies by Leads

◆ ◆ ◆

Nicholas Hiersche

Kyle N Hiersche

ABOUT THE AUTHORS

◆ ◆ ◆

As the CEO of a multi million-dollar company that he founded at the age of 15, Kyle Hiersche had an early start as an entrepreneur. Nicholas Hiersche, his brother and business partner, graduated from the University of Oregon College of Business. During his time at school, Nick helped Kyle build an idea into a successful company. Nick and Kyle were later asked to come back and speak to the graduating entrepreneurship class at the University of Oregon.

15 years later, the brothers own and operate six companies together doing business in seven different countries. Nick & Kyle are both licensed Realtors, real estate investors, entrepreneurs, authors, and of course...lead generators. While building multiple businesses that depend on leads, they have learned first hand how important lead generation is in today's market.

Nick is a Facebook Certified Media Planning Profesional, Facebook Certified Digital Marketing Associate, and Certified Google Ads Search Specialist. As the Founder of Follow The Lead Agency, he now manages advertising campaigns for Real Estate Brokerages, Law Firms, and Construction Companies.

After 12 years of experience and millions of their own dollars spent on lead generation, Nick and Kyle are sharing their insights in this book and hoping that you will *Follow The Lead*.

INTRODUCTION

◆ ◆ ◆

At the time this book is being published, it's the year 2020...a new decade. A decade that will usher in more advanced technology than ever seen before. The businesses and entrepreneurs that embrace this technology will have the key advantage in finding customers in the marketplace.

As of right now, almost every business has

the majority of its customers in one place every day...Facebook. Whether it's on Facebook itself, or the other platforms it owns such as Instagram, Whatsapp and a plethora of others. Facebook is where the customers are, so that is where we must be.

Thanks to Facebook, we all have the same ability to reach our customers using the Facebook advertising platform. It's an even playing field, whether you are a small business or billion-dollar corporation. We all have the same tools to use with Facebook for Business. The most advanced advertising platform ever created is available to all of us, no matter how small the company or budget. Isn't this amazing? Yes...and no.

It's precisely because everyone has access to

these tools that makes it so difficult to use them. We are all competing for the same customers, on the same platform, trying to outbid each other in a complex world of hidden algorithms.

With much of Facebook's "secret sauce" hidden to the public, no one knows the exact algorithms it uses to serve ads and determine pricing. We can study it and work with it better than others, but no one really knows what is happening behind the scenes besides Facebook. We are all in the same boat as far as that goes. Facebook likes to keep everyone chasing the dragon, letting you get close, but never letting you capture the formula.

So, how can we succeed in finding customers on a platform that everyone can use but no one can understand? This book will navigate through the process of utilizing today's technology for lead generation and management. We will be your guide on this journey to find new customers and new sales. We will *Follow The Lead*.

CHAPTER 1:

The Power of the Lead

◆ ◆ ◆

To live and die by the lead is the reality for many businesses in 2020. With so many competitors and so many ways for them to reach customers, we are forced to take more control of our sales and business. The days of letting customers come to us or pass by a "storefront" are long over. Now we must find the customers, get in front of them numerous times and then follow up consistently.

Lead generation tools and automated lead funnels are needed for many to succeed in today's landscape. Companies with these in place are sure to dwarf the sales of those without them. Finding customers online and converting them is the lifeblood of many businesses. It applies to selling products, real estate, services, and even getting people to come to a physical location. This is all originating online.

How we target these potential customers and what process we use to convert them will determine the success of our business. It is not enough to just sit around and respond to a few leads that come to us naturally. We must advertise to seek out the leads and capture them. Once the lead is captured, we must put them through an automated funnel to convert them and create follow up campaigns. The lead is where the power of our current and future sales lie.

CHAPTER 2:

A Lead Is Forever

◆ ◆ ◆

No lead should be taken for granted. Each lead must be nurtured until the time is right for them to convert into a customer. We paid for these leads with our own money and efforts, each one has value. Leads are never thrown away or wasted. A lead is forever. Years after a lead is generated, we should still be following up with them through automated campaigns.

When the time comes that our company's products or services are needed, we will be on the top of that customer's mind due to our persistence. Persistence created by automating a process and letting it work for us.

The power of the lead is not just driving more sales up front. Another power of the lead is that it remains an asset to our company as a future potential customer, whether we convert them right away or not. Circumstances change, things happen, some people may need to be followed up with at a later date. Some people may just see our consistency as professional and give us their businesses because of that.

There are many ways that we can remarket, convert and create revenue from leads at later dates. The key is that we need to go out and get the leads first! Once we have them, we must put them through an automated process. The funnel must come before the lead. Before we start advertising, we must first build the lead funnel to put them through. So, in the next chapter let's talk about this funnel that we will be putting the leads through…

CHAPTER 3:

The Funnel

◆ ◆ ◆

The all-mighty and powerful "funnel" is a mystery to some. Much like a Facebook pixel, it sounds like a daunting technology to understand and use. However, once we understand the basics of it, the rest is just settings and options. There are plenty of different CRM tools that can handle the front and back end of a lead funnel.

The key is to understand the general concept and how it works, then build one using the CRM of choice.

The "Funnel" is simply what we call the process of collecting leads, properly organizing them in a CRM and automating the sales process. The leads go into the top of the funnel and money comes out of the bottom.

In order to get leads into the top of our funnel, we are going to have to capture them through a landing page of some kind. We need a destination to send them to so they can see our offering and give us their information.

When advertising on Facebook they now have a lead form which collects their information before they hit a landing page. Whichever way we do it, we need to be able to capture their information to bring them into the top of the funnel and through to our CRM.

When putting them into our CRM, we make sure we tag them with where they came from and what they were interested in. This way, our CRM knows where to put them and how to follow up with them automatically.

For an effective funnel builder and CRM tool, check out our preferred partner, Funnld.com

FUNNEL DESIGN

LEAD SOURCES

LEAD CAPTURE

CATEGORIZED IN CRM

AUTOMATED LEAD NURTURE

LEAD CONVERSION

CHAPTER 4:

CRM

◆ ◆ ◆

A good CRM is a sales organization's best friend. Any business dealing with people, leads, or sales needs a great CRM platform. CRM stands for Customer Relationship Management which manages a company's interaction with current and potential customers. That essentially means it's how we keep track of everyone we are dealing with in the present and in the past.

Once we get a lead, we need to put them into our CRM platform. There are many different CRM platforms out there so we want to do our research to find the best one that works for our business. Some of the platforms are for specific industries like real estate but some are built to use in any industry.

The most important thing is that we're comfortable using the CRM we choose. Most of them have a free trial period or preview so we can determine if it's the right choice before purchasing. Once we get a lead, we keep track of them in the CRM and set up automatic follow up campaigns. Whether that campaign is emailing, texting automatically, or setting reminders to do follow up calls. Without this tool, businesses are just shooting in the dark chasing around clients or customers without any structure. A good CRM is a salesperson or sales organization's best friend.

I suggest checking out our preferred partner CRM, Funnld.

AD LEAD FLOW

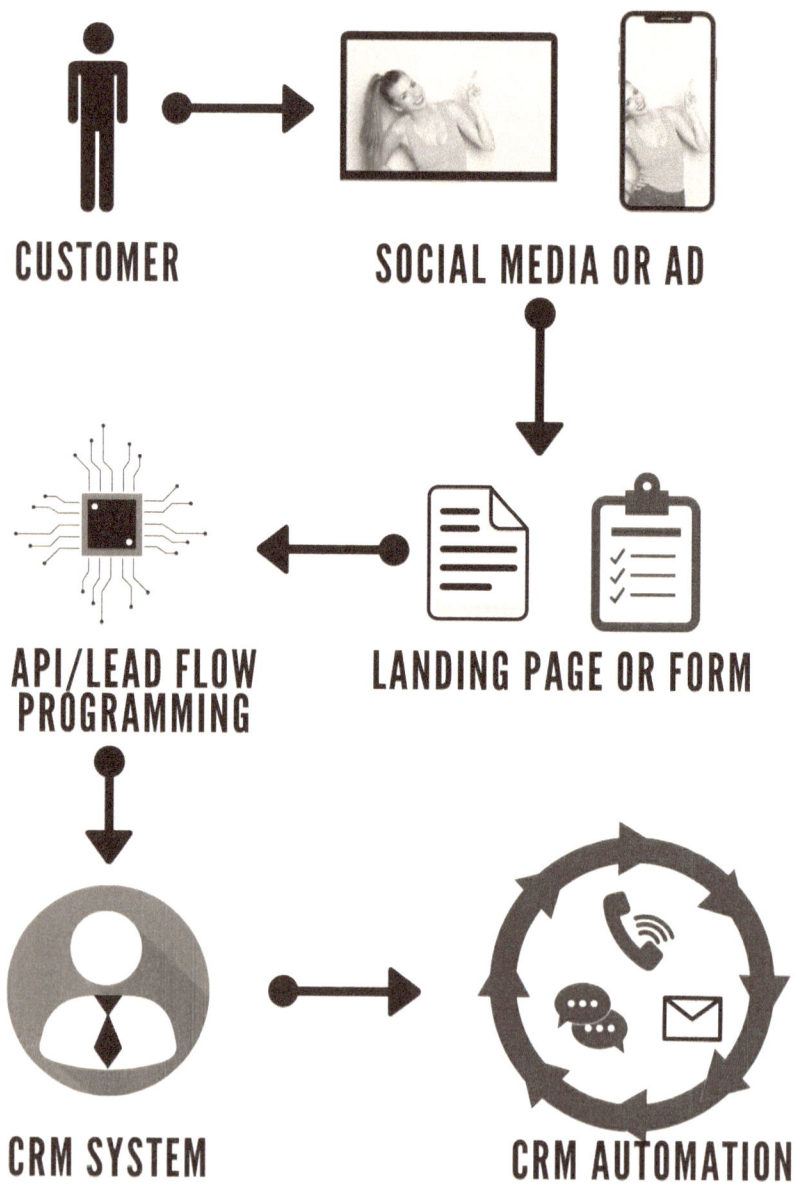

CUSTOMER

SOCIAL MEDIA OR AD

API/LEAD FLOW PROGRAMMING

LANDING PAGE OR FORM

CRM SYSTEM

CRM AUTOMATION

CHAPTER 5:

FREEMIUM

◆ ◆ ◆

The best way to convince potential leads to give out their information is the freemium model. Freemium essentially means to give the customer part of the experience for free, allowing us to collect their info as a lead. Once we have their info, we put them through the sales process or prompt them to purchase the premium version of the product or service offered.

The freemium model is key to many businesses, especially those that live online. In this day and age, users are not going to give their information to another website without seeing an immediate benefit. The advertisement and offering can be great, but is the immediate benefit there for the customer? What value are they receiving right now from giving out their information?

A traditional "free trial" is also somewhat of a freemium model but with so many options, customers prefer to use sites that don't require a credit card to start a trial. The goal is to bring them into the experience as soon as possible and push them to where we want them to go. We offer a premium option, or we push them through the sales process and into our CRM to organize and follow up with them.

When laid out like that, it doesn't seem so complicated does it? We advertise the lead to our freemium offer to capture them. Once we capture them, we push them through the sales process and stay organized and follow up by using our CRM. That is the goal of this book...and the freemium model is a great way to get there.

FREEMIUM

THE OFFERING

To engage with customers, we need something of value to offer for free in a simple and easy way.

THE IDEA

Once we have provided value to engage them, we can showcase our full idea (product or service).

THE UPGRADE

Once we have shown our basic free product or service, we offer an upgrade to the premium version.

THE REWARD

After providing an offer for free, we were able to engage. Now we turn that free engagement into a paid upgrade.

CHAPTER 6:

Facebook Lead Ads

◆ ◆ ◆

The easiest way to capture a lead on Facebook is by doing a Facebook lead ad. This allows the customer to sign up instantly with one click using pre-filled info that Facebook already has on file.

This means that instead of having an ad that goes to our site to capture a lead, we can capture them directly on Facebook with an easier, more seamless experience.

Anytime we are trying to capture leads, we want to make sure we have the least barriers to entry as possible. We want to enable the lead to give us their information in the quickest and easiest way possible. That includes making sure that our submit forms are above the fold on our websites and only collecting the bare minimum on the first sign up page. These are all steps that we can take on our own websites, but Facebook lead ads are even quicker with a one click sign up.

The only downside to a Facebook lead ad is that the leads are only as good as the data that the person gave to Facebook initially. Many times these leads have strange names, old phone numbers, etc. The lead is only as good as the info Facebook has so although it's an easier method to capture the lead, the data is not as quality.

There are upsides and downsides to Facebook lead ads like any other form of advertisement. This is where the practice of trial and error will help us decide if these lead ads are working for us better than others or not.

CHAPTER 7:

Advanced Facebook Ads

◆ ◆ ◆

Beyond using simple lead ad forms, Facebook has many options for us to target customers on Facebook and Instagram. Some of the most effective ads are the simplest ones. Often basic "memes" beat out professionally designed flyers when it comes to engagement. Facebook is a great tool because it allows us to load in our own pictures and text to try out different ads and see what works best.

Recently, Facebook rolled out a key feature that changed how Facebook Ads are done forever. Now with the Dynamic Ads feature, we can upload multiple images and multiple copies of texts and Facebook creates every possible combination of them. This generates hundreds of different ads by just uploading a few images and copy.

Once those ads are created, Facebook will serve them and track which ones work, automatically selecting the ones that get better results. This Dynamic Ads feature saves hundreds of hours by creating all possible ad combinations and learning to use the ones that work the best.

As a quick tip and best practice recommendation, we want to make sure we have the rights to the pictures we use. People do get sued over using images without permission on Facebook and Instagram ads and even posts for that matter. There are places to get licensed images from such as Canva.com and Shutterstock.com

When setting up any advertising campaign, we want to make sure we have the tools in place to track the effectiveness and results of the campaign. Since we are setting up a Facebook campaign, we need to track our results using the Facebook Pixel.

CHAPTER 8:

Pixels & Retargeting

◆ ◆ ◆

The term "Facebook pixel" seems complicated, but in reality it boils down to being a tracking device. When we get a lead from Facebook, we need to be able to track it all the way through our system knowing that it came from Facebook. This way we know how to treat that lead. The Facebook pixel will allow us to do that.

The pixel is placed in the code of the conversion website to track the origin and behavior of the visitors.

This data allows us to more effectively re-market to them later. That's what's happening when we browse items online and then get served ads for similar items afterwards. They tracked that behavior through cookies or a pixel and since we are interested in those items, they want to remarket and give us another chance to purchase.

Since a Facebook pixel allows us to see the behavior of the leads we're getting and where we are getting them from, we can use that data in other ways too. We can essentially create a profile of what our typical lead looks like and use that profile to target new leads who exhibit that behavior. It's amazing that Facebook can know so much about a person that it knows they should be our target before they do.

Facebook has amazing algorithms that are generally geared towards getting us the best results as an advertiser. They have more ways to do that than ever before which is why it's the most advanced advertising platform out there. We should always be using Facebook's data and algorithms in our favor by gathering as much as we can with a pixel to track, remarket and retarget.

CHAPTER 9:

Search Advertising

◆ ◆ ◆

Search advertising is the best way to generate a much more specific lead. These leads are already "searching" for the product or service, so putting ourselves at the forefront of the search will get us a greater conversion rate than a Facebook ad. However, depending on the keywords we are targeting, this can be much more expensive than Facebook.

The search advertising market is very competitive, with the winners sure to have a good chance of converting the leads. In this cut throat arena, we must make sure our copy and offering is enticing. We must make sure that our conversion landing page is fully optimized. We must be able to compete with the best of them.

Being able to bring our business to the forefront of search terms can be a very effective tool. When the ad campaign calls for it, we can utilize this tool to get specific leads for specific needs.

CHAPTER 10:

Putting It All Together

◆ ◆ ◆

Putting it all together is easier said than done. Funnels, CRMs, Facebook pixels, search ads...it seems like a lot. Most importantly, we need to grasp the general concept of how important leads are to our business. We need to find them, capture them, and use them properly.

There are a lot of tools to help us, like the

ones mentioned in this book and many others. If we are willing to learn, the knowledge is out there. These concepts and tools have a plethora of videos and articles online showing how to use them. As do the other tools and platforms that we weren't able to touch on in this book.

There are simply too many advertising opportunities to possibly fit them all into one book in 2020. There is incredible potential in the future of advertising and lead generation, but the game changes every day. We must stay on our toes at all times, learning and adjusting as we go.

Every year there's new technology that creates huge shifts in how we operate and do business. The landscape is always changing, but we will stay on course to reach the final destination. We will zig and zag, twist and turn, but we will stay on the path that leads to success. We will

Follow The Lead. ~

FOLLOW THE
LEAD AGENCY

◆ ◆ ◆

Nicholas & Kyle Hiersche are the Founders of Follow The Lead Marketing Agency. Follow The Lead specializes in using custom sales funnels to generate leads through online advertising. Clients include real estate brokerages, mortgage companies, contractors, and a law firm. To work with Nicholas Hiersche and the Follow The Lead Agency team, visit https://followthelead.agency

RESOURCES

◆ ◆ ◆

Here are some great resources that can help on your journey of building or expanding your business. There are plenty of books, blogs, webinars and seminars out there that you can find by doing your own research. These are just some of the resources we would recommend looking into.

.

BOOKS

◆ ◆ ◆

Never Had A Job: Living The Dream of Entrepreneurship - Kyle N. Hiersche

Build A Business, Not A Job! - Dave Finkel and Stephanie Harkness

Blue Ocean Strategy - W. Chan Kim and Renee Mauborgne

The Slight Edge - Jeff Olson

The Richest Man in Babylon - George Samuel Clason

As A Man Thinketh - James Allen

WEBSITES

◆ ◆ ◆

Digital Marketing:

FollowTheLead.Agency

Events & Seminars:

RealEstateLive.Events

CRM Technology:

Funnld.com

SPEAKERS

◆ ◆ ◆

Gary Vaynerchuk

Grant Cardone

Tony Robbins

Jim Rohn

Zig Ziglar

www.ingramcontent.com/pod-product-compliance
Lightning Source LLC
Chambersburg PA
CBHW021512210526
45463CB00002B/991